Dumb Jokes
for
Smart Kids

With cartoons by
Lucy Jordan

SCHOLASTIC INC.
New York Toronto London Auckland Sydney
Mexico City New Delhi Hong Kong

ISBN 0-439-30206-4

Published by Scholastic Inc., 555 Broadway, New York, NY 10012, by arrangement with Michael O'Mara Books Limited. SCHOLASTIC and associated logos are trademarks and/or registered trademarks of Scholastic Inc.

12 11 10 9 8 7 6 5 4 3 2   1 2 3 4 5 6/0

Printed in the U.S.A.   01

First Scholastic Book Club printing, April 2001

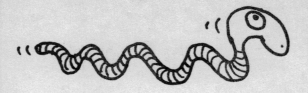

Contents

Animal antics   5

Crazy names   15

Doctor, doctor...   21

School side-splitters   29

Knock, knock jokes   35

Ghostly gags   43

Chortle, chortle   49

Funny food   57

Big, gray elephant jokes   63

What's so funny?   71

Waiter, waiter...   83

More laughs   91

Contents

Animal antics 7

Crazy names 15

Doctor, doctor... 21

Schoolside splitting 29

Knock, knock jokes 35

Ghostly crazy 43

Chuckle church 49

Funny food 57

Big, grey elephant jokes 63

What's so funny? 71

Water, water... 85

More laughs 91

Animal antics

**What do you get if you pour boiling
water down a rabbit hole?**
Hot cross bunnies.

What do you call a dog with a bunch of daisies on its head?
A collie-flower.

It's raining cats and dogs.
I know. I just stepped in a poodle.

How do you stop your dog from digging in the garden?
Take away his spade.

What happens when a frog's car breaks down?
It gets toad away.

What brand of gas do snails prefer?
Shell.

What game do cows play at parties?
Moosical chairs.

What is a cat's favorite TV programe?
Miami Mice.

What do you give a sick pig?
Oinkment.

What do you call a traveling flea?
An itch-hiker.

What do glow-worms eat?
Light snacks.

Mother kangaroo: I hate it when it rains and the kids have to play inside!

How many sheep does it take to make a sweater?
I didn't even know they could knit!

Why did the dachshund bite the woman's ankle?
Because he was short and he couldn't reach any higher.

**What do you get if you cross a parrot
with a centipede?**
A walkie-talkie.

**One goldfish swimming in a goldfish
bowl said to the other goldfish:
"Why do you keep following
me around?"**

**Why did the bald man paint rabbits
on his head?**
Because from a distance they
looked like hares.

**What do you get if you cross a
chicken with a cement-mixer?**
A bricklayer.

What do you call a penguin in the desert?
Lost.

Does your dog bite?
No.
Ow! I thought you said your dog didn't bite!
He doesn't. That isn't my dog!

How do you stop your dog from barking in the hall?
Put him in the garden.

**What animal always goes to bed
with its shoes on?**
A horse.

**How do you stop a skunk
from smelling?**
Hold its nose.

What is a bear's favorite drink?
Coca-Koala.

Who tells chicken jokes?
Comedi-hens.

**How do you find out where a flea
has bitten you?**
Start from scratch.

**What should you do if you find a
snake in your bed?**
Sleep in the closet.

What do you do with a sick wasp?
Take it to a waspital.

What is a slug?
A snail with a housing problem.

Has your cat ever had fleas?
No, just kittens.

What is a dog's favorite food?
Anything that's on your plate.

A man was amazed to see a dog buying meat for his owner in a butcher shop. Not only did he appear to check the quality of the meat, but he noticed that the butcher short-changed him, and growled until he was given the right money.

Intrigued, the man followed the dog from the shop and saw him help an old lady across the road with her shopping bags. The man then followed the dog to his owner's house and couldn't believe his eyes when the dog stood up on his hind legs to ring the doorbell.

The dog's owner came to the door, took the shopping from the dog and kicked him out into the garden. The man watching was horrified and called out to the owner,

"I can't believe you kicked that amazing dog - he does your shopping, checks your change, and even helps old ladies across the road!"
"I know," the owner replied, "but that's the third time this week that he's forgotten his keys."

What did one flea say to the other as they came out of the nightclub?
"Shall we walk home or take a dog?"

Why shouldn't you play cards in the jungle?
Because there are too many cheetahs.

What animal is best at baseball?
A bat.

What happened to the cat who ate a ball of wool?
She had mittens.

When is the best time to buy chicks?
When they're going cheap.

Crazy names

What do you call a woman with one leg shorter than the other?
Eileen.

**What do you call a boy with one foot
in the door?**
Justin.

What do you call a girl who gambles?
Betty.

**What do you call
a man wearing worn out clothes?**
Fred Bare.

What do you call a girl with one foot on either side of the river?

Bridget.

What do you call a man with a spade on his head?

Doug.

What do you call a girl with only one pants leg?

Jean.

What do you call a man who's a talented painter?

Art.

Who was the first underwater spy?

James Pond.

**What do you call a man who
can sing and drink soda at
the same time?**

A pop singer.

**What do you call a camel with
no humps?**

A horse.

**What do you call a camel with
three humps?**

Humphrey.

**What do you call a man
with a car on his head?**
Jack.

**What do you call a lady in
the distance?**
Dot.

**What do you call a girl
with a frog on her head?**
Lily.

**What do you call a man with numbers
down his front?**
Bill.

**What do you call a man in a pile
of leaves?**
Russell.

**What do you call a man
with a rabbit on his head?**
Warren.

What do you call a man who steals a lot?
Robin.

Who was Russia's most famous gardener?
Ivan Hoe.

What do you call a man with a seagull on his head?
Cliff.

I'M STUCK!

Doctor, doctor . . .

Doctor, doctor, I keep thinking I'm a telephone.
Well, take these pills and if you don't get better give me a call.

Doctor: You need glasses.
Patient: How can you tell?
Doctor: I knew as soon as you walked through the window.

Doctor, doctor, my head has flowers and trees growing out of it and people keep having picnics on me.
Ahhhh. I guess you've got a beauty spot.

**Doctor, doctor, I've got carrots
growing out of my ears.**
How did that happen?
I don't know, I planted onions.

**Doctor, doctor, I keep thinking
I'm getting smaller.**
Well, you'll just have to be
a little patient.

Doctor, doctor, I keep thinking I'm a fruitcake.

What's got into you?
Oh, you know, flour, butter, raisins . . . all the usual ingredients.

Doctor, doctor, I keep thinking I'm a goat.

How long have you felt like this?
Since I was a kid.

**Doctor, doctor, I think I'm
a bread roll.**
Oh, stop loafing around.

Doctor, doctor, I think I'm invisible.
Who said that?

**Doctor, doctor, my hair keeps falling
out. Can you give me something to
keep it in?**
How about this plastic bag?

**Doctor, doctor, I can't help
stealing things.**
Please take a seat.

**Doctor, doctor, my wife thinks
she's a clock.**
Are you sure you haven't been
winding her up?

**Doctor, doctor, can you give me
first aid?**
No, I'm afraid you'll have to
wait your turn.

**Doctor, doctor, I feel like a
pack of cards.**
Take a seat and I'll deal with
you later.

**Doctor, doctor, how can I
stop smoking.**
Try to avoid setting fire to yourself?

Doctor, doctor, I keep getting this stabbing pain in my eye when I drink a cup of tea.

Try taking the spoon out.

Doctor, doctor, I keep forgetting things.
When did this start happening?
When did what start happening?

Doctor, doctor, I think I'm a spoon.
Stay quiet, get lots of rest, and don't stir yourself.

Doctor, doctor, I keep seeing big pink monsters with purple spots.

Have you seen a psychiatrist?
No, just big pink monsters with purple spots.

Doctor, doctor, what's the best cure for flat feet.

A foot pump.

Doctor, doctor, I feel like an apple.

Don't worry, I don't bite.

Doctor, doctor, I think I'm a dustbin.

Don't talk such rubbish.

OOPs!

School
side-splitters

**Teacher: Name a legendary creature
that was half man and half beast.
Pupil: Buffalo Bill.**

Teacher: When was the Iron Age?
Pupil: Before they invented
drip-dry shirts?

**Teacher: What can you tell me about
the Dead Sea?**
Pupil: I didn't even know it was ill.

**Teacher: Why did cavemen paint
pictures on cave walls?**
Pupil: Because they couldn't
spell their names.

**Teacher: You should have been here
at 9 o'clock!**
Pupil: Why, what happened?

**Teacher: This homework is in your
father's writing.**
Pupil: I know, sir, I borrowed his pen.

What do music teachers give you?
Sound advice.

Teacher: Can you tell me where elephants are found?

Pupil: How could anyone lose an elephant?

Teacher: What was the Romans' most remarkable achievement?

Pupil: Learning Latin.

Teacher: If you had $5 in one pocket and $2.45 in the other, what would you have?

Pupil: Someone else's trousers on, miss.

**What word is always
spelled incorrectly?**

Incorrectly.

**Teacher: Can you name two days of
the week beginning with the
letter 'T'?**

Pupil: Today and tomorrow!

**Teacher: The ruler of old Russia was
called the Czar and his wife was
called the Czarina.
What were his children called?**

Pupil: Czardines?

What did the chicken study in college?

Eggonomics.

**Why did the thermometer go
to college?**

Because he wanted to get a degree.

Teacher: You have your shoes on
the wrong feet.

Pupil: They're the only feet
I have, miss.

**Pupil: Please miss, would you punish
someone for something they
didn't do?**

Teacher: No, of course not.

**Pupil: Oh good, because I haven't
done my homework.**

Teacher: If you had 50¢ in one pocket and you asked your Dad for another 50¢, what would you have?

Pupil: 50¢.

Teacher: You obviously don't know how to add.

Pupil: You obviously don't know my Dad!

Teacher: Give me a sentence with the word "indisposition" in it.

Pupil: I always play center because I like playing in dis position.

Parent: I'm worried about you being at the bottom of the class.

Child: Don't worry, Mom, they teach the same things at both ends.

Teacher: I wish you'd pay a little attention!

Pupil: I'm paying as little as I can, sir.

KNOCK KNOCK!

WHO'S THERE?

Knock, knock jokes

Knock, knock.
Who's there?
Albert.
Albert who?
Albert you'll never guess.

35

Knock, knock.
Who's there?
Tank.
Tank who?
My pleasure!

Knock, knock.
Who's there?
Boo.
Boo who?
Don't cry, it's only me.

Knock, knock.
Who's there?
Alex.
Alex who?
Alex plain later, just let me in.

Knock, knock.
Who's there?
Luke.
Luke who?
**Luke through the keyhole
and you'll see.**

Knock, knock.
Who's there?
Stan.
Stan who?
**Stan back, I'm going to break
the door down.**

Knock, knock.
Who's there?
You.
You who?
Did you call?

Knock, knock.
Who's there?
Snow.
Snow who?
Snow good asking me,
I can't remember.

38

Knock, knock.
Who's there?
Felix.
Felix who?
Felixtremely cold, can you let me in?

Knock, knock.
Who's there?
Watson.
Watson who?
Watson TV tonight?

Knock, knock.
Who's there?
Dozen.
Dozen who?
Dozen anyone know my name?

Knock, knock.
Who's there?
Hatch.
Hatch who?
Bless you.

Knock, knock.
Who's there?
Eddie.
Eddie who?
Eddie-body you like.

Knock, knock.
Who's there?
Liz.
Liz who?
**Lizen carefully, I'm only going to
say this once.**

Knock, knock.
Who's there?
Robin.
Robin who?
**Robin you, so hand over
your money.**

Knock, knock.
Who's there?
Hugh.
Hugh who?
Hugh wouldn't believe it if I told you.

Knock, knock.
Who's there?
Althea.
Althea who?
Althea later, alligator.

Knock, knock.
Who's there?
Canoe.
Canoe who?
Canoe hurry up and let me in?

Knock, knock.
Who's there?
Avenue.
Avenue who?
Avenue learned my name yet?

Knock, knock.
Who's there?
Dismay.
Dismay who?
Dismay be the wrong door, but
can you let me in anyway?

Ghostly gags

What is Dracula's favorite landmark?
The Vampire State Building.

What do you call a wizard from outer space?
A flying sorcerer.

How does a vampire cross the ocean?
In a blood vessel.

What is a monster's favorite game?
Swallow my leader.

What do polite vampires always remember to say?
Fangs very much.

Why did the skeleton go to the party?
Because he wanted a rattling
good time.

**Did you hear about the cannibal
with indigestion?**
He ate someone who disagreed
with him.

**When do ghosts play tricks on
each other?**
On April Ghouls' Day.

What is a ghost's favorite music?
A haunting melody.

What is Dracula's favorite pudding?
I scream.

**What do polite monsters say at
meal times?**
Pleased to eat you.

What do cannibals eat at parties?
Buttered host.

**What medicine do ghosts take
for colds?**
Coffin drops.

What do ghosts eat for dinner?
Ghoulash.

Why do vampires play poker?
Because the stakes are high.

What do short-sighted ghosts wear?
Spooktacles.

What do vampires put in their fruit salad?
Necktarines and blood oranges.

How did the two vampires fall in love?
Love at first bite.

What do you get if you cross Dracula with a hotdog?
A fangfurter.

Why does Dracula drink blood?
Because Diet Coke makes him burp.

Where do vampires keep their savings?
In a blood bank.

What do ghosts like on their roast beef?

Grave-y.

What does a monster eat when he's just been to the dentist?

The dentist.

Grrrr!

It's OUT!

What does a mailman deliver to ghosts?

Fang mail.

Chortle, chortle

What did the astronaut see in his frying pan?
An unidentified frying object.

Why did the biscuit cry?
Because his mother had been
a wafer so long.

Why is a forest always full?
Because trees a crowd.

Why did the dinosaur cross the road?
Because chickens hadn't evolved yet.

Do babies go on safari?
Not safari as I know.

Mommy, Mommy, what's a werewolf?
Be quiet Bill and comb your face.

Why did the man jump from the Empire State Building?
Because he wanted to make a hit on Broadway.

Why did the boy throw his clock out of the window?
To see time fly.

**What do traffic wardens have
in their sandwiches?**
Traffic jam.

**Why did the banana go out with
the prune?**
Because he couldn't find a date.

What race is never run?
A swimming race.

What kind of children live on the sea?
Buoys and gulls.

**If crocodile skins make a good pair
of shoes, what do banana
skins make?**
Good slippers.

Who invented the first plane that couldn't fly?
The Wrong brothers.

What lives under the sea and carries a lot of people?
An octobus.

FARES! PLEASE!

Which sixties pop group kills all known germs?
The Bleach Boys.

What did the Martian say to the gas pump?
Take your finger out of your ear when I'm talking to you.

What happened to the criminal contortionist?
He turned himself in.

What did one parallel line say to the other?
"It's a shame we'll never meet."

What cake is dangerous?
Attila the bun.

Why couldn't the bicycle stand up?

Because it was tyred.

What did the big chimney say to the little chimney?

You're too young to smoke.

Why couldn't the sailors play cards?

Because the captain was standing on the deck.

What do you give a sick bird?
Tweetment.

What has a bottom at the top?
A leg.

Pilot: Mayday! Mayday! Starboard engine on fire.
Ground control: State your height and position.
Pilot: I'm five foot nine and sitting in the cockpit.

What is worse than raining cats and dogs?
Hailing taxis.

What do you get if you cross a bridge with a car?
To the other side of the river.

Grrrrr!

Funny food

Why did the tomato blush?
Because he saw the salad dressing.

What kind of food does a racehorse eat?
Fast food.

Did you hear the one about the three eggs?
No?
Two bad.

Why should you never tell secrets in the produce section?
Because potatoes have eyes and beanstalk.

Why did the egg go to the jungle?
Because it was an eggsplorer.

Why did the peanut go to the police?
Because he'd been assaulted.

What's yellow and goes click?
A ballpoint banana.

What looks like half a loaf of bread?
The other half.

What do you call a mushroom who makes you laugh all day?
A fungi to be with.

How do you make a sausage roll?
Push it down the hill.

What's the fastest vegetable?
A runner bean.

How do you make an artichoke?
Strangle it.

What do Eskimos eat for breakfast?
Ice Krispies.

Why are cooks cruel?
Because they beat eggs and
whip cream.

Have you seen the salad bowl?
No, but I've seen the lunch box.

**A woman walked up to a man
and tried to tell him that he
had a leek sticking out of each ear.
"I'm sorry,' he said, 'I can't hear you.
I've got a leek stuck in each ear."**

What do dieting cannibals eat?
Thin people.

**What do you call a train
loaded with taffy?**
A chew chew train.

**What's white and fluffy and lives in
the jungle?**
A meringue-utan.

Why did the banana go to the doctor?
Because it wasn't peeling very well.

Why did the apple turnover?
Because it saw the swiss roll.

Big, gray elephant jokes

How does an elephant climb an oak tree?

He sits on an acorn and waits until spring.

**What did the grape say when the
elephant trod on it?**

Nothing, it just let out a little wine.

**What do you call an elephant
with no teeth?**

Gumbo.

**What's the difference between a
sleeping elephant and
one that's awake?**
With some elephants it's hard to tell.

Why do elephants live in the jungle?
Because they're too big to live
in houses.

**What do you get if you cross an
elephant with a biscuit?**
Crumbs.

**What's grey, has four legs,
and a trunk?**
A mouse going on holiday.

What do elephants sing at Christmas?
Jungle bells, jungle bells.

What's big, heavy, and gray, and has sixteen wheels?
An elephant on roller skates.

**What's the difference between a flea
and an elephant?**
An elephant can have fleas, but a flea
can't have elephants.

**What do you get if you cross an
elephant with a kangaroo?**
Great big holes all over Australia.

**Why did the elephant wear
sunglasses on the beach?**
Because he didn't want
to be recognized.

**What did the peanut say to
the elephant?**
Nothing, peanuts can't talk.

**What's the best way to catch
an elephant?**
Act like a nut and he'll follow
you anywhere.

**What is the same size and shape
as an elephant, but
weighs nothing?**
An elephant's shadow.

**Why did the elephant tie a knot
in his trunk?**
To remind himself not
to forget his hankie.

**Why did the elephant go backward
into the telephone box?**
He wanted to reverse the charges.

What is big, red, and has a trunk?
An elephant with sunburn.

What's big, gray, heavy, and wears glass slippers?
Cinderellaphant.

What is big, gray and protects you from the rain?

An umbrellaphant.

Jombo SIZE!

What's so funny?

My brother's built upside down. His nose runs and his feet smell.

What did the wall say to the plug?
Socket to me, baby!

**What did the policeman say
to his stomach?**
You're under a vest.

**Your stomach's too fat, you'll
have to diet?**
All right, but what color.

How do you make a bandstand?
Hide all their chairs.

**Mommy, Mommy, do I have to wash
my hands before playing the piano?**
Not if you only play the black notes.

Why shouldn't you tell jokes when you're ice-skating?
Because the ice might crack up.

Did you hear the one about the magic tractor?
It turned into a field.

What gets wetter as it dries?
A towel.

Why are you dancing with that jar of jelly?
It says, "Twist to open."

What type of monster eats the fastest?
A goblin.

Mommy, Mommy, can you see any change in me?
No, why?
I've just swallowed 5¢.

What nuts can be found in space?
Astronuts.

Why did the sailor grab a bar of soap when his ship was sinking?
He was hoping he'd be washed ashore.

What does the sea say to the sand?
Not much. It just waves.

What kind of bow is impossible to tie?
A rainbow.

Why do bees have sticky hair?
Because of their honey combs.

What do you call a sorceress who asks for lifts in cars?
A witch hiker.

How do you make an apple puff?
Chase it round the garden.

**Where does a general keep
his armies?**
Up his sleevies.

Why do wizards drink tea?
Because sorcerers need cuppas.

What is red and white?
Pink.

Why don't witches wear a flat hat?
Because there's no point in it.

What's red and green?
A tomato working part-time
as a cucumber.

**What happened when Moses
had a headache?**
God gave him some tablets.

**Why was the doctor working
on the highway?**
It needed by-pass surgery.

What did one eye say to the other?
There's something between us
that smells.

Why did the robber have a bath?
So he could make a clean getaway.

What did Cinderella say when she took her photos to be developed?
Some day my prints will come.

Can a shoe box?
No, but a tin can.

Why should you never put the letter "M" in the fridge?
Because it turns "ice" into "mice."

Where does your sister live?
Alaska
Don't worry, I'll ask her myself.

Why is it difficult to keep a secret on a cold day?
Because you can't stop your teeth from chattering.

Why didn't anyone take the bus to school?
Because it wouldn't fit through the door.

Why do witches get good bargains?
Because they like to haggle.

What is big, hairy, and flies to London faster than the speed of sound?
King Kongcorde.

Waiter, waiter...

Waiter, waiter, what's this fly doing on my ice cream?
Learning to ski I think, sir.

Waiter, waiter, bring me something to eat and make it snappy.

How about a crocodile sandwich, sir?

Waiter, waiter, how often do you change the tablecloths in this establishment?

I don't know, sir, I've only been here six months.

Waiter, waiter, this coffee tastes of mud!

That's perfectly natural, sir, after all it was only ground this morning.

Are you the same waiter who took my order?

Yes, sir.

My goodness, you've certainly aged well.

Waiter, waiter, what's wrong with this fish?

Long time, no sea, sir.

Waiter, waiter, how did this fly get in my soup?

It probably flew, madam.

Waiter, waiter, there's a fly in my soup!

That's OK, there's enough there for both of you.

Waiter, waiter, there's a fly in my ice cream!

Let him freeze to death, sir, it'll teach him a lesson.

Waiter: How did you find your steak sir?
Customer: Oh it wasn't difficult, it was just in between the potato and the salad.

Waiter, waiter, do you have frogs' legs?
Yes, sir.
Oh good. Can you hop over the counter and fix me a cheese sandwich?

HOP TO IT WAITER!

Diner: What's that?
Waiter: It's a tomato surprise.

Diner: I can't see any tomatoes in it.
Waiter: I know, sir, that's
the surprise.

**Waiter, waiter, there's a fly
in my soup!**
What do you expect for 50¢,
sir, a beetle?

**Waiter, waiter, your sleeve is
in my soup!**
Oh, there's no arm in it.

Diner: Is this chicken or onion soup?
Waiter: Can't you tell by the flavor?

Diner: No.
Waiter: In that case, sir, does it
make any difference?

Waiter, waiter, this egg is bad!
Don't blame me, sir, I only laid
the table.

**Waiter, waiter, why have you served me
a squashed apple pie?**
You said, "Step on it, waiter,
I'm in a hurry."

**Waiter, waiter, do you serve crabs
in this restaurant?**
We serve anyone, sir, please
take a seat.

**Waiter, waiter, this chicken's only
got one leg.**
Perhaps it's been in a fight, sir.
In that case bring me the winner.

Waiter, waiter, there's a fly in my soup.
That's all right, sir, we won't
charge you extra.

Waiter, waiter, do you have frogs' legs?

No, sir, I've always walked like this..

First customer: The service in this restaurant is terrible!

Second customer: I know, but the food is so bad, I don't mind waiting for it.

Waiter, waiter, this soup tastes funny!

Then why aren't you laughing, sir?

Waiter, waiter, there's no chicken in this chicken pot pie!

Would you expect to find dog
in a dog biscuit, sir?

Waiter, waiter, there's a small slug in my salad!

I do apologize, sir, would you like
a bigger one?

Waiter, waiter, what's this fly doing in my soup?

It looks like backstroke to me, sir.

Waiter, waiter, I'm in a hurry - will my pancake be long?

No, sir, it will be round.

Waiter, waiter, there's a spider in my soup. Get me the manager!

That won't do any good, sir,
he's afraid of them too.

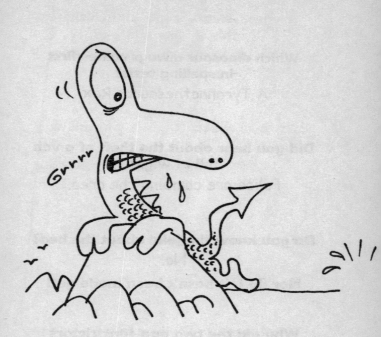

More laughs

What do you call a one-eyed dinosaur?

D'youthink'esaurus.

**Which dinosaur always comes first
in spelling tests?**

A Tyrannathesaurus Rex.

**Did you hear about the theft of a van
full of wigs?**

Police are combing the area.

Do you know the joke about the bed?

No.

Nor do I, it hasn't been made yet!

**Why did the two boa constrictors
get married?**

They had a crush on each other.

**Why did the cowboy jump
off the wagon?**

Because he got stage fright.

Do you play the piano by ear?
No, I've always found it easier
to use my hands.

**Why was the little Egyptian
girl upset?**
Because her daddy was a mummy.

Which vegetable is good at pool?
A cue-cumber.

"I'd like to be included in your next edition," said the man on the phone to the *Guinness Book of Records*. "Why, what have you done?" came the reply. "I've completed a jigsaw in just under a week and on the box it says three to five years."

How do Eskimos dress?
As quickly as possible.

Why is the sky so high?
So birds don't bump their heads.

What is big, green, bad-tempered, and wears ripped clothes?
The Incredible Sulk.

Why did the tonsils get dressed up?
Because the doctor was taking them out.

How did the detective find Quasimodo?
He followed a hunch.

How do you get rid of a boomerang?
Throw it down a one-way street.

What do you call small rivers that run into the Nile?
Juveniles.

Teacher: What do you want to be when you grow up?

Boy: I want to follow in my father's footsteps and be a policeman.

Teacher: I didn't know your father was a policeman?

Boy: He's not, he's a burglar.

What do you call a flying policeman?

A helicopper.

What is a crocodile's favorite game?

Snap.

SNAP!

NO THANKS!